THE WORLD AROUND YOU

COLORS IN NATURE

by

Christianne Jones

PEBBLE

a capstone imprint

Published by Pebble, an imprint of Capstone
1710 Roe Crest Drive, North Mankato, Minnesota 56003
capstonepub.com

Library of Congress Cataloging-in-Publication Data
Names: Jones, Christianne C., author. Title: Colors in nature / by Christianne Jones. Description:
North Mankato, MN : Pebble, [2022] | Series: The world around you | Audience: Ages 5-8 |
Audience: Grades K-1 | Summary: "From vibrant red flowers and clear blue skies to big brown
trees and buzzing yellow bees, color is everywhere in nature. Interactive, rhyming text and
bright photographs bring the bold colors of nature to young readers in this picture book"—
Provided by publisher. Identifiers: LCCN 2021028232 (print) | LCCN 2021028233 (ebook) |
ISBN 9781663976710 (hardcover) | ISBN 9781666325157 (paperback) | ISBN 9781666325164
(pdf) | ISBN 9781666325188 (kindle edition) Subjects: LCSH: Color in nature—Juvenile
literature. | Colors—Juvenile literature. Classification: LCC QC495.5 .J6575 2022 (print) | LCC
QC495.5 (ebook) | DDC 535.6—dc23 LC record available at https://lccn.loc.gov/2021028232
LC ebook record available at https://lccn.loc.gov/2021028233

Editorial Credits
Editor: Christianne Jones; Designer: Brann Garvey; Media Researcher: Svetlana Zhurkin;
Production Specialist: Laura Manthe

Image Credits
Shutterstock: Amit Erez, top 12, Andrey Krepkih, spread 2-3, Artens, (flowers) Cover, Avdeenko,
(G) 29, blueeyes, (M) 29, Bruce MacQueen, top left 5, Christian Musat, bottom right 30, Dennis
Jacobsen, middle right 5, Diliana Nikolova, spread 20-21, Dominic Gentilcore PhD, (H) 29,
Edwin Godinho, top 19, Elizaveta Kirina, top left 11, evaurban, top 26, Evgeny Dudarev, top
right 30, fpfoto, middle left 5, Gayvoronskaya_Yana, 7, Henk Bentlage, top right 16, irin-k, (A)
29, jo Crebbin, bottom 22, Keat Eung, top 22, Konstanttin, (O) 29, korson, bottom 11, Landscape
Nature Photo, 27, LecartPhotos, middle 23, Lifestyle Graphic, middle 19, Luc Mena, top left
23, LucVi, 13, manfredxy, (L) 29, Maren Winter, 17, matushaban, middle 4, Mircea Costina, top
left 18, mozz.art, bottom right 10, Olga Danylenko, spread 8-9, Ondrej Prosicky, bottom right 4,
Pablesku, (J) 29, Paul Nicholson, top left 4, Picture This Images, (D) 29, Piotr Krzeslak, bottom
16, Procy, spread 24-25, Roger Givens, top right 4, rsooll, (F) 29, Rudmer Zwerver, bottom right
5, Sergei Drozd, (C) 29, Sergey, bottom 6, Serhii Brovko, (I) 29, ShadeDesign, bottom 26, Stefano
Politi Markovina, (rainbow) Cover, Steve Byland, bottom left 4, Super Prin, bottom left 5, Susan
Flashman, top right 5, tharathep lomchid, bottom 12, Thinker360, middle right 30, Tyler Olson,
(N) 29, Vaclav Matous, top left 16, Vaclav Sebek, bottom left 30, Volodymyr Burdiak, top left 30,
vvvita, spread 14-15, Yatra, bottom 18, You Touch Pix of EuToch, top left 10, yul38885, (E) 29,
yuris, top 6, Yuriy Kulik, (K) 29, yyama, (B) 29

Special thanks to Sveta Zhurkin and Dan Nunn for their consulting work and help.

A WORLD OF COLOR

What a boring place the world would be,
without lots of colors for you to see.
Open your eyes. Look around.
Nature has many colors to be found!

FLYING COLORS

Red birds and **brown**—
flying colors galore!
Spot all the colors
you know and adore!

red

orange

brown

yellow

green

blue

pink

purple

white

gray

black

Delicious **red** berries shine in the sun.

A small **red** bug is looking for fun.

Blooming **red** tulips adorn a flower bed.

Where else in nature can you spot **red**?

Still **blue** water looks like nature's mirror.

The bright **blue** sky could not be clearer.

But there's more to see than just these two.

Where else in nature can you spot **blue**?

A spiky **green** cactus thrives in the heat.

A quiet **green** frog eyes a yummy treat.

Green insects are part of the outdoor scene.

Where else in nature can you spot **green**?

A **yellow** flower attracts **yellow** bees.

A burst of **yellow** hangs from the trees.

A small **yellow** snail is slow and mellow.

Where else in nature can you spot **yellow**?

An evening storm passed with lightning and thunder,
leaving behind this stunning **orange** wonder.
After the fierce storm, the sky settled down.
Where else in nature can **orange** be found?

A tree is home to a **brown** owl
and a **brown** pine cone.
A prickly **brown** hedgehog hunts alone.

A curious **brown** prairie dog will soon head back down.

Where else in nature can you spot **brown**?

A **gray** wasp nest is buzzing with action. A soft **gray** koala is an adorable attraction.

A **gray** seal is resting as storm clouds darken the day.

Where else in nature can you spot **gray**?

A field of **purple** flowers is a spectacular sight.

The setting summer sun casts the perfect light.

Look all around you. Spin in a big circle.

Where else in nature can you spot **purple**?

Gorgeous **pink** coral lives in the ocean.

A determined **pink** spoonbill takes off in motion!

There are **pink** birds and **pink** bugs, so stop and think.

Where else in nature can you spot **pink**?

Stars are scattered across the **black** sky.

How many constellations can you spy?

Be patient and look. Lie on your back.

Where else in nature can you spot **black**?

White polar bear cubs play in the snow.

A fluffy **white** dandelion is ready to blow.

The **white** snow sparkles, shiny and bright.

Where else in nature can you spot **white**?

Animal Color Quiz

1. What color is an elephant?

2. What color is a baby chicken?

3. What color is a tiger?

4. What color is a polar bear?

5. What color is an orca whale?

The answers can be found on page 30.

Flower Fun Quiz

Look at all these bright flowers. Can you sort them into color groups? How many of each color did you find?

The answers can be found on page 31.

Animal Color Quiz Answers

1. An elephant is **gray**.

2. A baby chicken is **yellow**.

3. A tiger is mostly **orange** with **black** stripes.

4. Polar bears are **white**.

5. An orca whale is mostly **black** with some **white**.